Virtual Reality for Rehabilitation

Healing Without Physical Limitations

Table of Contents

Chapter 1. Introduction

In this groundbreaking Special Report, we invite you to explore the astonishing intersection of technology and medical care—Virtual Reality for Rehabilitation: Healing Without Physical Limitations. Prepare to engage with an accessible yet deeply insightful narrative, expertly crafted to bridge the gap between highly complex technology and clear, understandable prose. Witness how breakthroughs in virtual reality (VR) technology are challenging boundaries, fusing seamlessly with rehabilitation to transform lives in ways never thought feasible. This report not only presents the era-defining advancements in therapeutic techniques and empathetic computing, but also ushers our readers into a hopeful future where resilience transcends the constraints of physical limitations. Intriguing, isn't it? Brace yourself, as this fascinating read is only the beginning! So, why wait? Reserve a fascinating journey into the realm where technology meets healing today!

Chapter 2. The Intersection of Virtual Reality and Rehabilitation

As we inch closer to the precipice of technological innovation, the marriage of Virtual Reality (VR) and rehabilitation comes into focus as a triumphant symbol of progress. The amalgamation of these two areas has given birth to a novel approach, capitalizing on the immersive power of VR to overcome traditional hurdles in rehabilitation therapy.

2.1. Harnessing the Power of Immersive Technology

The driving force behind VR's efficacy in rehabilitation lies in its immersive capabilities. VR stands as a potent conduit to transport users into alternate realities, where they can interact with virtual objects as if they were real. This all-encompassing nature of the technology provides a fertile ground for rehabilitating patients, as it places them in meticulously designed environments suited for their therapeutic needs.

VR's therapeutic potential is not restricted to mere physical rehabilitation. In fact, it has begun to affect strides in mental health treatments as well. By re-creating distressing situations in a controlled setting, mental health professionals manipulate these virtual environments to help patients overcome anxiety disorders, post-traumatic stress disorder (PTSD), and various phobias.

2.2. Breaking Barriers in Therapeutic Techniques

The cutting-edge technology VR brings to pass an array of intricate interventions that challenge conventional therapeutic techniques. Motor rehabilitation, for instance, utilizes this technology to offer an immersive and engaging approach. Rehabilitative clinicians craft tailored virtual environments that encourage patients to perform designated movements or tasks.

In practice, this means a patient recovering from a stroke might engage in VR exercises that simulate actions like picking up a coffee cup or throwing a ball. As the patient maneuvers through the virtual realm, they receive immediate visual feedback that mirrors their actions.

Such VR simulations offer an unprecedented level of intermediation in therapeutic observations. Moreover, the ability to modulate obstacle difficulty gives therapists an unparalleled degree of control. Tailored VR experiences encourage repetition of tasks, thereby fostering motor learning in a manner that surpasses traditional modes of exercise.

2.3. Possibilities in Post-Stroke Rehabilitation

Stroke patients frequently grapple with multiple functional impairments, such as mobility, motor control, and spatial perception issues. Here lies another possible application of VR, its use in formal post-stroke rehabilitation.

One of the practical applications of VR in this scenario is immersive gait training. Stroke survivors exhibiting hemiplegic gait can "walk" in a virtual environment, thus encouraging neuroplasticity and motor function recovery in a safe, stimulating setting. Likewise, VR tools can assist in traditional exercises like range-of-motion and strengthening drills. These exercises, coupled with the immersive nature of VR, provide a potent combination that can hasten recovery.

2.4. Embracing Empathetic Computing

Empathetic computing proffers an intriguing adjunct to VR in rehabilitation. It encourages the creation of technologies that sense and react to the emotions and psychological states of users. This approach can be monumental in developing personalized treatment plans based on the user's experience of pain, stress, and even their cognitive load.

Utilizing empathetic computing in rehabilitation adds an extra layer of flexibility to treatment plans. For patients with chronic pain, VR environments can be adapted to their individual pain thresholds, thereby enhancing the therapeutic potential of this technology. Furthermore, VR combined with this emotional insight can foster the concept of 'positive distractions' in patients, providing significant relief to those with severe pain.

2.5. A Future without Constraints

Virtual reality harbors the capacity to push the boundaries of what is currently conceivable in rehabilitation. This marriage of technology and medical care is poised to transcend limitations, offering the promise of a future where therapeutic intervention can overcome the physical constraints of yesterday.

On a concluding note, the potential of VR in rehabilitation is profound. It presents remarkable possibilities for revolutionizing the landscape of medical rehabilitation and mental health therapy. By merging the immersive capabilities of VR with the empathetic understandings of patient needs, we take an enormous leap towards a future that no longer separates healing from technology. We are poised on the brink of a transformative era, where technology no longer merely aids healing; instead, it becomes an integral part of the healing process itself.

Chapter 3. Decoding Virtual Reality: An Overview

The advent of virtual reality (VR) was an epoch marked by the application of immersive technology for entertainment, gradually extending to areas like education, military, and medicine. Its ability to create and control a three-dimensional, computer-generated environment that could be explored interactively offered transformative possibilities, the full potential of which is yet to be realized.

3.1. A Journey into Virtual Reality

Virtual Reality is a technology that projects users into a digitally synthesized environment, making them feel present in the virtual world. Typically, VR is experienced through head-mounted displays, specifically designed goggles that completely block out all external light and display a three-dimensional image or video. Additional components might include handheld controllers, gloves designed to provide haptic feedback (sense of touch), and omnidirectional treadmills for simulating motion.

Users can interact with the virtual environment in an extraordinarily intuitive manner. This interaction is often facilitated by tracking systems in the gloves or handheld devices that map physical movements directly onto the VR world. In essence, VR offers an immersive, multi-sensory, and interactive experience that attempts to simulate physical presence in a non-physical world.

3.2. The Building Blocks of Virtual Reality

There are three key components integral to a high-fidelity VR experience: a VR headset, a robust tracking system, and powerful rendering software.

Firstly, the VR headset, typically equipped with a high-resolution display and wide field-of-view, is the primary conduit between the user and the virtual environment. It shuts off the real world and replaces it with a digital universe.

Secondly, the tracking system, commonly implemented using cameras or sensors mounted around the perimeter of the play space, carefully maps the user's movement in the real world onto their avatar in the virtual world.

Lastly, the rendering software, which often works seamlessly with powerful computer hardware, builds and displays the virtual world. It generates user-responsive environments and objects within fractions of a second.

These components work in harmony to create and maintain the illusion of an alternate reality.

3.3. Virtual Reality vs Augmented Reality vs Mixed Reality

It's worth distinguishing between Virtual Reality, Augmented Reality (AR), and Mixed Reality (MR) - terms often used interchangeably but actually represent distinct technologies within the reality-virtuality continuum.

In VR, the user is completely immersed in a computer-generated reality, or virtual environment. AR overlays digital information onto the real world. Under AR, the user stays in the real-world environment while interacting with virtual objects.

MR is the merging of real and virtual worlds to produce new environments and visualizations where physical and digital objects co-exist and interact in real-time.

3.4. Real-World Applications and Potential

Virtual Reality has been deployed across multiple sectors with varying levels of success. Its applications can be found in the gaming industry for an immersive and interactive gaming experience. It is also used in real estate, where potential homebuyers can take a virtual tour of the property.

In education and training, VR has shown promise in providing a new medium for learning. Whether it is for the training of pilots, surgeons, or military personnel, VR can simulate situations that would otherwise be prohibitively costly, dangerous, or impracticable.

Virtual Reality has also found utility in groundbreaking therapeutic interventions, particularly in physical rehabilitation and psychological treatments. This is where the areas of healthcare and VR intersect, opening up possibilities for innovative and transformative applications.

3.5. Virtual Reality in Healthcare and Rehabilitation

Traditionally, healthcare practitioners have relied upon hands-on physical therapy and other standard rehabilitation techniques - effective but not always efficient methodologies dependent on several factors like physician's expertise, patient's resilience, or financial viability etc. Through VR, the opportunity to transform how patients rehabilitate has become plausible.

In VR-assisted rehabilitation, patients wear VR goggles to immerse in a virtual environment that simulates real-world exercises typically done in physical rehabilitation.

The burgeoning field of VR rehabilitation exhibits a considerable range of applications, from helping stroke patients regain motor function and managing chronic pain, to getting soldiers back on their feet after combat injuries. Virtual Reality has shown promise in delivering effective and measurable rehabilitation therapies, heralding a new epoch in the way we approach physical rehabilitation.

As we delve deeper into the pages of this report, we'll examine specific instances of VR's applications in rehabilitation, unraveling the intricacies that make this technology as promising as it is challenging – continually pushing the boundaries of what's possible in the realm of healing without physical limitations.

Chapter 4. Innovative VR Therapies in Practice

Cardiovascular training, relaxation therapy, balance assessments, motor skills improvement – one would imagine these rehabilitation activities being conducted in a traditional physical space with specialized equipment. Yet, with innovative VR therapies, these sessions are loosening their tether to physical constraints, striding boldly into an era of digital and immersive therapy sessions.

4.1. A Shift in Paradigm: Virtual Reality in Rehabilitation

The consensus in the medical community is clear: VR has revolutionized rehabilitation. Rather than relying solely on physical therapeutic methods, innovative VR applications allow for immersive, interactive experiences that effectively engage patients during their rehabilitation process. By integrating virtual reality systems, rehabilitation centers can provide more personalized and intensive therapeutic sessions, offering patients enhanced physical, cognitive, and even psychological healing opportunities.

As opposed to merely simulating reality, virtual reality can augment it, creating an interactive environment according to specific needs, be it to challenge a user's balance, test their cognitive functions, or simply allow for stress relief in immersive, peaceful settings. Versatile as it is innovative, virtual reality adapts to serve a range of therapeutic goals.

4.2. Lifelike Environments: Enhancing User Engagement

In rehabilitation contexts, maintaining patient engagement and motivation can often be a tough challenge. Enter VR - its immersive, three-dimensional environments significantly enhance patient motivation during rehab sessions. Instanced virtual environments couple auditory, visual, and sometimes haptic feedback to create settings that stimulate patient focus while maintaining an atmosphere of entertainment and fun. From navigating virtual labyrinths to exercising in simulated landscapes, VR-equipped therapists have more tools than ever before to engage their wards in purposeful activity.

Let's consider a simple exercise, such as a balance game, where the patient needs to shift their weight to control a ball's movement on a physical platform. A VR application can translate this experience into an engaging game, where a participant can navigate their virtual avatar across challenging terrains, collecting rewards along the way. This motivates patients to perform traditionally mundane exercises with higher levels of engagement and enthusiasm.

4.3. Neuromuscular Rehabilitation: A Leap Forward with VR

Perhaps where VR's transformative aspects shine the brightest are in neuromuscular rehabilitation. Motor-relearning concepts are fundamental in neuro-rehab, often involving the repetitive execution of specific movements aimed at restoring motor function. Virtual reality offers interactive and flexible environments wherein these tasks transform into engaging exercises, obfuscating the rigors of repetition with the allure of the virtual world.

Patients recovering from a stroke, often face motor deficits and have to relearn essential functions such as walking or grasping objects. With VR, these exercises become scenarios of manipulation in an unconventional world. Patients can reach and grasp virtually generated objects, determining their strategy, speed, and approach technique. The data procured in such interactive schemes provide invaluable insights, helping clinicians devise ongoing strategies for rehabilitation.

4.4. Confronting Phobias: Virtual Exposure Therapy

Anxiety disorders, including phobias and panic conditions, are some of the major challenges faced in the field of mental health. Virtual reality, in this respect, has made significant contributions. Its quintessential application is present in the form of Virtual Exposure Therapy (VET). Employing state-of-the-art VR technology, patients are exposed gradually and safely to their fear triggers in controlled virtual surroundings. These sessions provide the necessary therapeutic structure wherein patients challenge their phobias, gradually acknowledging and overcoming them over time, while under constant supervision.

For example, a person suffering from acrophobia, the fear of heights, can be gradually exposed to ascending virtual heights while standing on solid ground. As patients progress, therapists adjust the exposure intensity, allowing patients to confront their fears incrementally. This VR application expedites therapies that would otherwise depend on actual scenarios for exposure, thereby limiting their reach and application.

4.5. The Road Ahead: Challenges and Opportunities

Despite its transformative impact, the integration of VR into standard therapy comes with its own set of challenges. Potential issues such as cybersickness, attributable to visual-vestibular conflicts, the high cost of VR equipment, and the need for patients to adapt to novel technology, are real concerns that need to be tackled for the full utilization of VR's potential in rehab therapy.

Yet, the future of VR in rehabilitation is rife with possibilities. Recent advancements in wearable sensor technology, haptic feedback devices, and AI algorithms promise to further enhance therapeutic VR experiences. By relentlessly evolving alongside emerging technologies, VR continues its journey towards greater interactivity, immersion, and subsequently, better rehabilitation outcomes.

VR technology has emerged as a game-changer in rehabilitation therapy, bridging gaps, bringing improvements, and opening doors that many thought impossible mere years ago. Innovative VR therapies have begun to reshape the field of rehabilitation, offering a promising hint at a future where healing, like the technology it employs, knows no bounds.

Chapter 5. Virtual Reality and Neurological Rehabilitation

The bold strides of medical technology bring us today to a juncture that was earlier the realm of science fiction. The world of Virtual Reality (VR), no longer merely a conduit of grand adventures and epic narratives for video gamers, now stands on the precipice of groundbreaking healthcare applications.

5.1. The Crossroads of Virtual Reality and Neurology

What exactly makes Virtual Reality so promising within the sphere of neurological rehabilitation? A considerable part of the answer lies in the brain itself. The magnificent human brain, through centuries of evolution, has developed an extraordinary capacity known as neuroplasticity. Neuroplasticity refers to the potential of our neural pathways to reorganize and adapt themselves based on our experiences. And this is precisely what VR taps into, enabling new avenues for rehabilitation through its immersive interface.

Virtual Reality creates an environment that effectively blurs the lines between the physical and digital world. When an individual interacts with the VR environment, it stimulates the brain in novel ways, forging fresh neural pathways and strengthening existing networks. This encodes learning at an accelerated pace, enabling patients to regain lost capacities and even discover new ones.

5.2. VR in Action: Stroke Rehabilitation

One of the most notable applications of VR in neuro-rehabilitation can be seen in stroke therapy. Stroke victims are often plagued with deficits in motor control, which can profoundly impede daily activities. Conventional physical therapy, while beneficial, is hindered by the physical limitations and frustrations experienced by patients.

Virtual Reality, however, reimagines the therapeutic landscape. Therapy sessions turn into interactive gaming experiences, as patients undergo tasks in the virtual space using VR headsets and handheld controllers. Each movement in the game is mirrored in reality, tricking the brain into believing that the body is moving more than it is. This embodiment illusion in VR contributes significantly towards motivating patients and fostering an optimistic outlook towards their recovery.

5.3. Advancements in VR: Neurological Amputations and Prosthetics

Another burgeoning area in Virtual Reality is the management of phantom limb pain (PLP) among amputees. Many amputees experience severe pain in limbs that no longer exist, which has been attributed to the brain's confusion due to the sudden disappearance of vital sensory input. VR seeks to alleviate this through the concept of 'virtual embodiment.'

Using a combination of Virtual Reality and artificial intelligence, a digital representation of the missing limb is created in the VR environment and connected with the individual's neural signals. The individual can visualize and control their lost limb in the VR space. This advanced form of biofeedback, by offering an immediate visual reference, can aid in rewiring the brain's neural circuitry and reduce phantom limb pain.

5.4. VR Rehabilitation Applications for Children

While adult rehabilitation dominates the discussion on Virtual Reality's implications, its potential applications for pediatric neuro-rehabilitation are equally noteworthy. VR can distance children from the clinical environment's often intimidating circumstances, supporting therapy through play-based virtual interactions. A child can be transported to a fantastical world where therapy becomes a playful and engaging experience rather than a routine chore, making children more receptive to the treatment process.

5.5. The Journey Ahead – Potential Challenges and Ethical Considerations

Despite the promise, the integration of Virtual Reality into healthcare does not come without its challenges. Not everyone can tolerate VR, as it can induce cybersickness in some users. Affordable and accessible VR healthcare solutions require further developments in technology, and there is a critical need for broader clinical trials to establish evidence-based guidelines on VR therapies.

In addition, ethical considerations about patient data handling and privacy in VR systems are paramount. As VR technology develops and expands in healthcare, professionals will need to engage in ongoing discussions regarding these aspects.

In conclusion, the visionary blend of Virtual Reality and neurological rehabilitation is poised to be a game-changer in healthcare. The efficacy of VR in retraining the brain, motivating patients, and enhancing recovery experiences is proving increasingly significant. While we acknowledge the potential hurdles, the multidimensional benefits of VR are propelling this technology into becoming an integral part of the rehabilitation toolkit of the future. As we stride into this exciting new landscape, the phrase 'the Art of the Possible' has never been more apt.

Chapter 6. Physical Rehabilitation: Taking Steps into the VR World

The dawning of the twenty-first century ushered in an era of unprecedented progress in our understanding of science, medicine, and technology. Among the many advancements, one that has emerged as particularly promising is Virtual Reality (VR), a technology that has far-reaching implications in various domains, including the field of physical rehabilitation.

6.1. VR Defined

VR involves the use of computer technology to create an interactive, simulated environment. Unlike traditional interfaces, which usually allow actions or manipulation via the mouse or touch, VR places the user inside an experience. Rather than viewing a screen, the user is immersed in a 3D world and able to interact with the environment in ways that feel, to a significant degree, incredibly realistic.

6.2. How VR Works in Rehabilitation

Physical rehabilitation can be a grueling journey, replete with significant challenges. It requires the patient to repetitively perform exercises to recoup lost functions, often against the resistance of pain, muscle weakness, and demoralization due to slow progress. The challenge is twofold: to encourage the patient to keep up with the rehabilitative exercises and to chart progress accurately to ensure the chosen strategy's effectiveness. This is where VR shows remarkable promise.

VR environments, through the use of immersive simulations, can coax the brain into believing that it is actually executing the task at hand. This "embodiment" phenomenon is a key trigger in the brain's plasticity (the ability to adapt to changes), which forms the cornerstone of rehabilitation.

6.3. Real World Application: The VR Treadmill

Take, for example, a typical treadmill exercise. Typically, it may be challenging for a stroke patient to walk due to muscle weakness and impaired balance. However, using VR and a specially designed treadmill (like the VirtualRehab platform), the patient can be made to walk on a beautiful beach, complete with the sights and sounds. The patient, therefore, isn't focused on the exhausting nature of the task but is instead immersed in the serene landscape, reducing perceived exertion and enhancing exercise intensity.

By using VR, physical therapy transforms into something captivating, even entertaining, thus subtly encouraging more practice. Furthermore, the VR system could provide real-time feedback about how well the patient is performing the exercises, giving the physiotherapist a measurable and objective assessment that was previously difficult to achieve.

6.4. Case Studies: VR for Rehabilitation

There have been several case studies that demonstrate VR's efficacy in different physical rehabilitation contexts. One such example is the study where VR was used to improve balance and mobility in patients recovering from Stroke. Patients who integrated VR along with conventional physiotherapy showed significant improvement compared to those who only underwent traditional rehabilitation.

Another case embarked upon using VR to facilitate motor recovery after spinal cord injuries. Participants, despite experiencing severe limb function deficits, were able to gradually regain movement and mobility using carefully curated and personalized VR training.

6.5. A Bright Future Ahead

With the promise that VR holds, every advancement brings us closer to a future where physical limitations do not define the boundaries of our capabilities. As the technology continues to refine and the body of clinical evidence grows, VR will undoubtedly become a mainstay in rehabilitation, helping countless individuals regain their independence and improve their quality of life.

While we are still at the junction where VR's potential is gradually unfolding, each milestone reached gives us a promising glimpse into a future where resilience decidedly outpaces the constraints of our physical world. The marriage between technology and medical care, with VR at its epicenter, heralds an epoch where healing is no longer confined to the physical world but spans across a realm where possibilities are as far-reaching as the technology enables.

Chapter 7. Psychological Rehabilitation: Healing the Mind with Virtual Environments

The realm of psychological rehabilitation, hitherto characterized by traditional talk-based therapies, medication regimes, and cognitive-behavioral techniques, is being strikingly revitalized by the advent of virtual reality technology. As we immerse ourselves in this transformative arena, we open our minds to the wondrous capabilities of VR, enabling us to explore the seemingly limitless potential of this medium for mental health healing and empowerment.

7.1. The Advent of Virtual Therapy

As technology advances at unprecedented rates, the traditional barriers of psychological therapy—namely, geographic restrictions, financial resources, and stigma—begin to diminish. Hailing the era of virtual therapy, eye-opening successes of VR are being witnessed around the globe, reshaping how we perceive and practice psychological rehabilitation.

Virtual reality-based therapy isn't a novel concept. Its history traces back to the 1990s when it was used as exposure-based therapy to treat fear and anxiety disorders. These early endeavors were promising; however, the technology at the time was cumbersome and expensive. As we fast-forward to the present, VR technology has become more mature, affordable, and widespread, effectively infiltrating the mainstream and redefining the sphere of psychological therapy.

7.2. Therapeutic Modalities Through Virtual Engagement

Interactive technologies such as VR engage users on a remarkably immersive level, fostering a sense of place and presence that results in deeper emotional engagement. The core of this transformative therapy revolves around two primary techniques: virtual exposure therapy (VET) and cognitive training.

Virtual exposure therapy leverages the immersive and emotive nature of VR to expose patients to situations or environments that may trigger anxiety or distress. By carefully controlled and graded exposure to these virtual environments, patients can confront and gain mastery over their fears and anxieties within the safety parameters defined by the therapeutic setting. From fears of spiders to traumatic memories from warfare, VET serves as a powerful tool for therapists.

Cognitive training, on the other hand, emphasizes the development and strengthening of cognitive abilities. It helps individuals rebuild cognitive skills impaired through mental health conditions like depression, PTSD, or even as a result of brain injury. Activities can range from memory games for Alzheimer's patients to virtual reality social cognition training for people with autism.

7.3. Virtual Reality and Post-Traumatic Stress Disorder (PTSD)

Virtual reality has shown promise in combating one of the most debilitating psychological disorders - PTSD. Using a technique called Prolonged Exposure Therapy, patients are reintroduced gradually to the traumatic memories in a safe environment. The therapy, now performed in a VR setup, allows individuals to re-experience the trauma within a controlled virtual environment. This immersive approach helps to disrupt the cycle of avoidance and fear, promoting healthier coping mechanisms.

Professionals monitor patients' physiological responses to these virtual scenarios, adjusting the intensity based on patient comfort and progress. This detailed, interactive, and dynamic therapeutic process has reaped encouraging results, significantly reducing PTSD symptoms and aiding in the recovery process.

7.4. Virtual Reality and Phobias

VR has also proven beneficial in the treatment of specific phobias. The phobic individual is gradually exposed to their fear in a controlled virtual environment, thus allowing them to confront and overcome their fears without the immediate real-world risks. For example, acrophobia (fear of heights) is often treated using a virtual environment that gradually simulates a higher and higher altitude, making it progressively challenging.

7.5. The Transformative Impact on Depression

Depression can lock sufferers into a negative thought pattern and a distorted self-image. Through VR therapy, a technique known as Embodied Self-Compassion is proving revolutionary. It allows patients to self-soothe by embodying a comforting figure and expressing compassion towards their virtual self. These sessions have shown promising results, with patients reporting an increase in self-compassion and a decline in self-criticism.

7.6. Looking Beyond Traditional Therapies

VR therapy's potential in psychological rehabilitation appears boundless; from modulating pain in burn victims by providing escape through calming VR programs to helping addicts cope with cravings by replicating triggering environments and coaching healthier reactions.

Virtual Reality for rehabilitation is truly more than meets the eye. It holds the potential to revolutionize treatment protocols, imbuing hope into countless individuals globally. This is only the tip of the iceberg. It is a fascinating journey towards understanding and healing the human mind using technology—an adventure teeming with promise and optimism.

Indeed, the panorama of psychological rehabilitation is experiencing a profound upheaval as it stands on the precipice of this technological breakthrough. So, are we ready to step into this brave new world of healing and hope?

Prudent advancements in technology, combined with relentless human ingenuity and empathy, will continue to steer the ship of psychological rehabilitation towards uncharted realms of possibilities and prospects. As this chapter closes, another opens, promising an enthralling adventure replete with innovation, hope, and healing.

Just as the infinity of the human psyche intrigues us, the horizons of Virtual Reality in psychological rehabilitation, likewise, seem limitless. Therefore, we must continue to explore, learn, and grown in this burgeoning field, with the hope that our efforts would serve to breakthrough the barriers of psychological anguish and unshackle the constraints of the human spirit.

Chapter 8. Consumer Perspectives: Personal Healing Journeys with VR

Virtual reality (VR) technology has seen impressive use in various industries but its true potential has been unleashed in the world of medical rehabilitation. Its uses in rehabilitating patients with stroke, managing chronic pain, or aiding in physical therapy sessions have brought a paradigm shift in treatments and therapy.

8.1. Foray into Virtual Reality for Rehabilitation

The journey of an individual through their rehabilitation can be a slow, arduous task, and technology has sought to make that journey easier. Virtual reality, one of the emerging technologies of the new age, has carved its path in this sector showing promise in aiding recovery faster than conventional methods. The simultaneous interaction with a virtual world can expedite healing while enhancing the experience of therapy sessions.

8.2. The Melding of VR and Rehab: Taking the Leap of Faith

Beginning with understanding the technology at an abstract level, users often express an initial apprehension, curiosity coupled with doubt. But with the first use, these immediate concerns recede. Users report being surprised by the intuitive and immersive experience VR provides. The ease of use and the prospect of trying something novel often brings about an enthusiasm previously unseen in traditional therapy sessions.

8.3. Shedding the Physical Limitations

One of the greater benefits of VR is its ability to create virtual environments tailored to individual needs. Whether it's recreating the functions of lost limbs for an amputee or progressively complex moving targets for a stroke victim, the limits are defined only by the creativity and understanding of the software developers and therapists involved. There can be an embodiment of virtual limbs, tuning into the mental and physical state of the user, effectively removing any barriers imposed by their physical existence.

8.4. Experience of Emotional Healing

Relief and joy are often the first emotions experienced through the use of VR in rehabilitation. Therapists have noted time and again the cathartic effect of using VR as an extension to physical therapy. By virtually performing activities that bodily limitations may restrict, users have reported reduced anxiety and an unprecedented upliftment of the spirit. Subsequently, a recurring pattern is the establishment of confidence and will-power in patients.

8.5. Complementing Conventional Therapies

Despite the numerous benefits, the integration of VR into regular therapy sessions remains a crucial point of scepticism. Observations, however, indicate that when applied appropriately, virtual reality can complement conventional therapies, enhancing the efficiency and effectiveness of treatments. It aids to efficiently track the progress and objectives, thus providing measurable milestones that can motivate patients towards swifter recovery.

8.6. Looking Ahead: Navigating Possibilities

The prediction of the trajectory of development in VR rehabilitation relies on the pioneering researchers, technologists and therapists who experiment and innovate. The virtual environment is only bound to grow more immersive and realistic, potentially expanding its usefulness in rehabilitating patients. Continuous progression in technology, accessibility, and reach of VR into more hands is the ultimate objective, providing healing without constraints.

8.7. Learning from Real-life Stories: Evidentiary Support

Feedback and testimonials from patients across the globe bear witness to the transformative power of virtual reality. These stories showcase VR's potential to not just act as a tool for rehabilitation but also as a catalyst to rebuild the lives affected by physical limitations. The patients' tales of regaining mobility, their confidence resurging, and their lives improving point towards the hope offered by this technology.

As we delve deeper into the juncture of VR and rehabilitation, it's clear that consumer perspectives signify a shift in perception towards the broadening scope of medicine. Bridging the gap between technology and treatment, it becomes evident that the application of VR in rehabilitation encompasses more than physical recovery. VR's potential for emotional healing and its ability to complement traditional treatments affords consumers a newfound agency in their journey towards recovery. The intersection of VR with rehab is not just a groundbreaking breakthrough; it represents a new frontier of possibility in healthcare.

Chapter 9. Future Horizons: Upcoming Advancements in VR Rehabilitation

In envisioning the future of VR rehabilitation, it's not unrealistic to forecast a momentous change. Much like how hearing aids or artificial limbs were once seen as groundbreaking, VR is now generating a similar stir within the medical community. As this influential technology continues to ascend and amass increasingly intricate computational capabilities, we foresee an explosion of dynamic and innovative applications within rehabilitation.

9.1. Stochastic Environments and Increased Complexity

The leap from static and predictable VR environments to dynamic, stochastic environments represents an imminent and significant step in VR rehabilitation. Human motion in a real-world environment isn't lived in a vacuum—rather, we adapt to chaotic and ever-evolving surroundings. Accordingly, the next generation of VR applications will incorporate unpredictable elements into rehabilitation exercises, reflecting real-world complexity and challenging patients' adaptability in a safe and controlled manner.

These stochastic environments will test not only physical capabilities but also cognitive functions, enhancing neuroplasticity and promoting full recovery. As this aspect of VR application development progresses, we'll see increasingly personalized and detailed virtual world simulations tailored to an individual patient's needs and rehabilitation progress.

9.2. Implementation of Biofeedback

In the heart of our upcoming VR rehabilitation advances stand biofeedback-based adaptive systems. Biofeedback, defined as the process of gathering real-time information about the body's physiological state, is already integrated to a limited extent in existing technologies. But in the future, we anticipate unfolding more exhaustive and sophisticated applications.

Using sensors to monitor patients' heart rate, muscle activity, sweat gland activity, or brainwaves, VR systems will then modulate environmental settings or task difficulty based on these direct physiological signals. This kind of responsive, adaptive therapy could deepen the integration of VR in physical as well as neurological rehabilitation programs, engendering more personalized and effective treatments.

9.3. AI-driven Personalized Rehabilitation

Take a moment to envisage a future where Artificial Intelligence (AI) plays a monumental role in patient recovery. AI technology can learn patients' behaviors, monitor their progress, and shape therapy programs to their unique needs. Coupled with biofeedback, it can infer the individuals' load tolerance from physiological cues and adjust the VR environment accordingly.

Research institutes are already developing AI-driven VR systems that intuitively understand the user's movement patterns, therapy goals, and possible limitations. Future VR systems, following this trajectory, could offer a much finer-grained adaptation to each patient's needs, resulting in improved therapeutic outcomes that are beyond what we can currently anticipate.

9.4. Integration of Augmented Reality (AR)

Whereas VR creates an entirely virtual world for users, Augmented Reality (AR) integrates digital elements into our existing environment. As the line between VR and AR continues to blur, exciting opportunities are gradually emerging for rehabilitation.

In an AR enhanced environment, patients will be able to overlay virtual objects on their real-world surroundings and interact with them for therapeutic purposes. Whether it's maneuvering a wheelchair through a digital obstacle course placed in a patient's living room, or using simulated objects for cognition-enhancing tasks, AR can offer a more enriched, immersive and convenient rehabilitation option.

9.5. Tele-rehabilitation and Remote Monitoring

Tele-rehabilitation, the ability to conduct therapy in the comfort of one's home while monitored remotely by a healthcare provider, is an increasingly viable future scenario. VR applications will not only make home-based rehabilitation more effective but also enable real-time, remote monitoring of patients' progress.

A future where physical therapists can guide patients through a VR rehabilitation exercise from miles away comes with many potential benefits. It could drastically reduce hospital readmission rates, improve patient compliance, and make healthcare more accessible for those in rural, remote areas.

9.6. Therapeutic Video Games

Another prospective area of continued development lies in therapeutic video games and simulations. A combination of compelling game design and therapeutic exercise could greatly increase patient commitment to their rehabilitation programs. The use of gaming elements in a VR framework can turn monotonous therapy into a fun and engaging activity, thus improving the likelihood of consistent adherence.

In conclusion, the future of VR rehabilitation glimmers with potential – the convergence of VR, AR, AI algorithms, biofeedback technology, and gaming designs hold unparalleled therapeutic possibilities. The sector certainly awaits many technical and medical challenges. Still, as technology blooms exponentially, a world where physical limitations are transcended through virtual possibilities is not merely a fantasy—it's an oncoming reality. The future of rehabilitation lies not in the confines of our physical world, but in the infinite expanse of the virtual.

Chapter 10. Challenges and Ethical Considerations in VR Rehabilitation

For those diving into the world of Virtual Reality (VR) rehabilitation, it is essential to first consider the challenges and ethical considerations we may encounter. Despite the vast revolutionary progress in technologies, multiple obstacles remain. To fully comprehend the predicotal nature of such technological accomplishments, we must overcome these challenges and navigate the ethical landscape with care.

10.1. The Technical Challenges

VR, despite being frontier technology, isn't impervious to technical glitches and mishaps. As a considerably new technology, it's still going through its teething phase. Application and integration of VR into healthcare sectors require immense technological expertise, coupled with a high-level understanding of healthcare practices and regulations.

Firstly, there's the challenge of hardware design and software optimization. While strides have been made in creating sleek and user-friendly hardware, problems persist. The current state of hardware provides an incomplete or interrupted experience, causing additional stress or confusion to patients already dealing with health issues.

Furthermore, the issue of software optimization comes into play. The creation of realistic, immersive virtual environments is a complex endeavor, requiring both high-grade computation resources and advanced programming skills. Additionally, algorithms must be meticulously designed to track and render movements in real-time without lag or errors.

10.2. Privacy and Data Security

As with any new technological solution applied in a sensitive context such as healthcare that involves collecting patient data, privacy becomes a genuine concern. How can we ensure patients' sensitive information remains private and secure when employing VR-based rehabilitation methods?

In VR, data isn't limited to medical records or demographic information. It also includes tracking data captured during VR sessions—data that could potentially reveal significant insights about a patient's condition or abilities. The matter of ensuring data privacy while harnessing its value is a challenge demanding immediate addressal, and the solution involves a delicate balance of ethical responsibility and technological capability.

10.3. Accessibility of VR Solutions

Accessibility is a multidimensional issue concerning VR technology. It lies at the intersection of multiple stakeholders—the tech developers, healthcare providers, and the patients themselves. Not only does it refer to affordability but also to usability and availability.

The current costs of VR solutions, both hardware and software, are sky-high, limiting wide-scale availability. Usability also becomes a concern as not all patients are technologically inclined or capable of navigating intricate interfaces. For VR to be truly transformative, it must be accessible to a broader audience—regardless of their tech-savvy or financial abilities.

10.4. Equity of Access

Given the nascent stage of VR, globally, the distribution of VR resources is concentrated within developed regions. This uneven distribution raises serious concerns about the equity of access. Will these cutting-edge technologies be restricted to patients in developed countries, leaving behind those in less fortunate circumstances?

While progress is being marked with each passing day, the question of whether these advancements will ever become global is still very much in the air.

10.5. Ethical Concerns

The new terrain of VR rehabilitation sways into the unseen territory of ethical dilemmas. The capacity of VR to provide an alternative, immersive reality opens up trials of manipulation and informed consent. There are indications that VR can affect memory, cognition, and perception of reality—not always positively.

Informed consent becomes a pressing matter. The degree to which VR will affect an individual varies, making it hard to provide a complete consultation regarding the risks and benefits.

10.6. Health Risks

Despite the numerous therapeutic applications of VR, it isn't devoid of health risks. Many users report motion sickness, disorientation, and eye strain after using VR, which are often termed as 'cybersickness'. These side effects may pose additional health risks or discomfort to patients, especially those already in a higher state of vulnerability due to existing health conditions.

Careful, evidence-based protocols and guidelines must be developed to minimize these potential negative effects while maximizing the therapeutic benefit.

Despite its numerous challenges and ethical considerations, VR rehabilitation holds tremendous promise for the future of healthcare innovations. It offers an opportunity to surmount physical limitations in the therapeutic process and pioneer a transformative approach to patient care. However, the path to its wide acceptance and implementation demands comprehensive solutions to these issues. Vigilance, research, and ethical guidelines developed hand in hand with technical advancements will open new horizons in this exciting intersection of technology and healing.

Chapter 11. Virtual Reality Rehabilitation: A Vision for the Future

Capitalizing upon the rapidly evolving certainty of today, the interplay of virtual reality (VR) and rehabilitation is pushing the outer limits of what we once deemed possible.

11.1. The Voyage to Virtual Reality

The roots of virtual reality enjoy a history that is longer than one might anticipate. Beginning with immersive artworks and panoramic murals meant to mesmerize the viewer, VR has honed its form through multiple decades of technological iterations. Today's VR technology finds its genesis in the 19th century with stereoscopic photos and viewers. Arcane as those initial steps may be in the rearview mirror of present understanding, they paved the path to our current zenith of VR innovations. As computing technology progressed, these layered panoramas evolved into interactive experiences, envisioning a world not restrained by the physical.

11.2. VR: The Digital Medicine

As VR entered the spheres of medicine and rehabilitation, it shattered the barriers posing challenges to traditional forms of treatment. VR, nestled at the intersection of comfort and novelty, leverages the power of computer-assisted advancements aimed at tackling some of the most daunting medical issues. Mirroring real-world environments digitally, it produces a replicative space where users can trial, error, and ultimately master life skills in a safe, controllable, and malleable virtual world without the typical stressors.

11.3. Reinventing Rehabilitation

Considering rehabilitation, VR brought forth an innovative spin on traditional modalities. Our realities are multisensory experiences; dense networks of stimuli challenging our cognitive and physical abilities continuously. For individuals recovering from traumatic injuries, strokes or long periods of immobilization, reintegrating into the fluidity of daily life presents unparalleled difficulties. However, virtual reality extends a rope of hope. Through comprehensive VR simulations, patients experience a realistic, safe, and controlled environment to adjust to their new 'normal', evoking a sense of freedom to fail and learn without repercussions.

11.4. Mapping the Neural Pathways

Scientific research in neuroplasticity—the brain's capacity to forge new connections, has illuminated an integral aspect of VR's efficacy in rehabilitation. It is no secret that our brains embody immense plasticity. This inherent flexibility allows the formation of new neural connections in response to learning, or in this case, re-learning. A virtual environment offers a visually rich, 3D, and interactive milieu that stimulates the sense of presence and participation, thereby activating more extensive areas of the brain.

11.5. Empathy, Connection, and Feedback

VR goes beyond mechanical treatment by introducing a deeply empathetic approach to rehabilitation. VR-based therapy sessions, in essence, are treated as collaborative experiences rather than authorative sessions. The patient is invited to explore, attempt, and overcome virtual tasks in a liberating environment free from judgment and laden with supportive feedback. Embedded within this approach is the customization factor – VR therapy programs can be attuned to each patient's needs, facilitating personal breakthroughs on the path to healing.

11.6. Trials and Successes: Case Studies

Multiple institutions globally are integrating VR into their rehabilitation programs, with encouraging outcomes. For instance, the USC Institute for Creative Technologies, through their "Bravemind" program, developed VR Exposure Therapy to treat veterans battling PTSD. Similarly, VR has been utilized in pain management, cognitive rehabilitation post-stroke, and even helping children with cerebral palsy increase their motor functioning.

11.7. VR and the Future of Rehabilitation

Considering these extensive applications, it's clear that VR is setting a fresh trajectory for the future of rehabilitation. However, it is still a budding branch in the vast tree of therapeutic procedures. A combined effort across medical fields, tech companies, and regulatory bodies is required to harness its full potential. As more intensive research and policy-level adjustments ensue, VR-based therapies will undoubtedly burgeon into a mainstream therapeutic model, transforming lives, and reinstating the joys of a functional existence for those who brace the trials of physical constraints.

Indeed, we find ourselves amidst the dawn of an era where rehabilitative medicine transcends the tactile and fuses with the virtual. Technology continues its ceaseless march, with VR at the tip of the spear, pioneering a future where healing is liberated from physical constraints and infused within the digital wonder of our creative imagination. The magic of VR lies not in the technology itself but in its capacity to serve as a conduit of hope, resilience, and limitless evolution.